Prescription Scriptures

Vol. 4 Children

(A Heritage of The Lord)

Photographed by: Sunni Barbosa-Reeves and Tommy Reeves

Prescription Scriptures

Vol. 4 Children

(A Heritage of The Lord)

ISBN-13:
978-1723539565

ISBN-10:
1723539562

Published by GODLYGirl Entertainment.

789 Hammond Dr. Suite # 2701

Sandy Springs GA, 30328

(Referenced from the King James Bible)

Search Sunni Barbosa on Amazon.com

Please make a small commitment to google GODLYGirl Ent.

And leave us a one-word review, we appreciate your feedback.

Thank You for Supporting Positive Media!

These teachings have been inspired by:

Pastor Monique

&

Walter Rice

(World Outreach Christian Center)

And

Ernest Leonard Ministries

May God Himself continue to reward your obedience

Thank you!

This is a book that allows you to save time, in a time of need by taking you straight to the children's scriptures of the Bible without the search. Nothing is too big for God.

All you gotta do is believe.

This is what you will need to do:

Speak it into Existence! These Scriptures are to be recited as many times as needed, the more the better. (There are no words more powerful then Gods Words, use them to stab and poke holes in the devil's butt!

Now, Doesn't that sound like FUN?)

The enemies torment our children just as much as they torment us,
if not more.
Don't take it personal! We must continuously wipe our children's slates clean.

1. Anoint your children's heads with anointing oil on a daily and nightly basis, pray over them, decree and declare what you want them to be;
   Example: bind to their souls from the kingdom of heaven the spirits of obedience, joy, peace, giving, love, humility, diligence, discernment, unity, the will of GOD etc.

Cast out every negative spirit; Example: cast out the spirits of rebellion, separation, jezebel, homosexuality, confusion, lust, disobedience, depression, laziness, stealing, addiction, lying, brain fog and generational curses etc.

2. Believe! (True Faith) Believing that God is able according to His own words.

3. Be Proactive! Don't wait for things to go wrong in your children, take the necessary steps to ensure that certain things don't go wrong whenever possible.

4. Communicate! Communicate! Communicate! When you are open and honest with each other this leaves little to no space for the enemy to enter.

5. Place hedges of protection around your children and no matter what type of behavior they display, always see for them what GOD sees.

6. Teach your children to write their very own personal prayers, have them to pray as much as possible, prostrating on their faces, this is so much better then making them take meds that alter their behavior and mood.

7. Spend real quality time with your children teaching them about GOD, his expectations and promises and teaching them how to truly fight for their own life and salvation. At some point it will be their own responsibility and not yours and we want for our children to be able to defeat whatever challenges may come their way. Set the best example you can possibly set for your children, they are not just going to do **what you tell them to do but they are also going to do what you do, they are always watching.**

Proverbs 22:6

Train up a child in the way he should go: and when he is old, he will not depart from it.

Leviticus 19:29

Do not prostitute thy daughter, to cause her to be a whore; lest the land fall to whoredom, and the land become full of wickedness.

1 Timothy 5:8

But if any provide not for his own, and specially for those of his own house, he hath denied the faith, and is worse than an infidel.

Ephesians 6:4

And, ye fathers, provoke not your children to wrath: but bring them up in the nurture and admonition of the LORD.

Proverbs 13:24

He that spareth his rod hateth his son: but he that loveth him chasteneth him betimes.

In other words (Spare the rod and spoil the child, if you love your children you must discipline them and yes this means spanking too.)

3 John 1:4

I have no greater joy than to hear that my children walk in truth.

Matthew 19:14

But Jesus said, suffer little children, and forbid them not, to come unto me: for of such is the kingdom of heaven.

In other words (Push the children towards God and Jesus, do not stand in the way of them.)

Proverbs 29:15

The rod of reproof give wisdom: but a child left (to himself) bringeth his mother to shame.

In other words (Get in your child's business.)

Proverbs 20:11

Even a child is known by his doings, whether his work (be) pure, and whether (it be) right.

Isaiah 54:13

And all thy children (shall be) taught of the LORD; and great (shall be) the peace of thy children.

Proverbs 23:13

Withhold not correction from the child: for (if) thou beatest him with the rod, he shall not die.

1 Samuel 1: 27-28

27 For this child I prayed; and the LORD hath given me my petition which I asked of him: 28 Therefore also I have lent him to the LORD; as long as he liveth he shall be lent to the LORD. And he worshipped the LORD there.

Colossians 3:21

Fathers provoke not your children (to anger), lest they be discouraged.

Psalms 112:1-2

1 Blessed is the man who fears the LORD, who greatly delights in his commandments! 2 His offspring will be mighty in the land; the generation of the upright will be blessed.

Isaiah 61:9

Their offspring shall be known among the nations, and their descendants in the midst of the peoples; all who see them shall acknowledge them, that they are an offspring the LORD has blessed.

Deuteronomy 4:40

Therefore, you shall keep his statutes and his commandments, which I command you today, that it may go well with your children after you, and that you may prolong your days in the land that the LORD your GOD is giving you for all time.

Exodus 20:12

Honor thy father and thy mother: that thy days may be long upon the land which the LORD thy GOD giveth thee.

Proverbs 20:7

**The righteous who walks in his integrity-
blessed are his children after him.**

Isaiah 65:23

They shall not labor in vain or bear children for calamity, for they shall be the offspring of the blessed of the LORD, and their descendants with them.

Psalms 115:14

The LORD shall increase you more and more, you and your children.

Psalms 127:3

Lo, children (are) an heritage of the LORD: (and) the fruit of the womb (is his) reward.

Made in the USA
Monee, IL
19 April 2021